Little Book of

Dogs

D1410459

NATIONAL LIBRARY OF AUSTRALIA

Published by the National Library of Australia
Canberra ACT 2600
Australia

Title: Little book of dogs.

ISBN: 9780642276698 (pbk.)

Series: Little book series

Subjects: Dogs--Poetry.
                Dogs in art.

Other Authors/Contributors:
                National Library of Australia.

Dewey Number: A821.0080362977

Compiled by Maree Bentley and Jo Karmel
Designed by Amy Cullen
Printed by Imago

Front Cover Illustrations: see pages 3 and 43.
Back Cover Illustration: see page 3.

Contents

My Dog
Jack Davis

You foolish creature charging in
To flop in my chair with your lop-sided grin,
You chew my shoes and eat my socks:
I'm sure your head is made of rocks.
I plant, you dig my flowers and lawn,
You bark when the roosters crow at dawn.
You chase the baker, you bit the rector,
But you seem to adore the bill-collector.
Chaos comes with you through the door—
You are a clown and not much more.

But when I sit by the fire at night
And the world is mostly sleeping,
My thoughts caught up in fancied flight,
Then gently you come creeping.

You sit and stare at me above you,
Your tongue-tip soft as a feather,
And I stretch my hand to prove I love you—
A man and his dog together.

James Wigley (1918–1999), *I Am Rill's Dog* 1977; ink, texta and pastel, coloured drawing; 15.0 x 12.4 cm; Pictures Collection; nla.pic-vn3642986-s14

Relativity
William Hart-Smith

The main reason why dogs
Love to sit in cars
is because
when a dog's inside
a car doesn't move

When the doors
of the small intimate room
with master and mistress in it
close

the room bucks
and barks and makes
most unusual noises
and odours

then houses get up and run
trees get up and run
posts get up and run
and telegraph poles

in fact everything does

With his nose thrust out
bang in the eye of the galloping wind
his right ear streaming
like a strip of rag in a gale

he for a change can sit still
chin on the window-sill

and let the world do all the running
about

(above)
S.T. Gill (1818–1880), *Native Dogs* 1849; wash drawing; 15.7 x 23.8 cm
Pictures Collection; nla.pic-an2376811

(p.9)
Charles H. Kerry (1858–1928), *Preserved Dingoes on Display* (detail) 1894–1895
sepia-toned photograph; 15.0 x 20.0 cm; Pictures Collection; nla.pic-an3366506

the visitor
Miriel Lenore

Irrunytju the dingo is back
she fed him as a pup
thought he'd left for ever

'bring him meat
get his rug
he might need water'

he sits on her foot
his strangled yowl a conversation
& leaves the meat

why has he come if not for food?
surely he's a father now out bush?
perhaps he missed us after all

that night black clouds & wind
thunder a mighty storm
Irrunytju sleeps on his blanket

in the morning he's gone

she checks each track
recalls their desert walks
epiphanies he helped her see

she only gave occasional food
he never was her pet
they always met as equals

both still choose to be free

Dogs and God
Geoff Page

That bikie with his
girl as pillion,
that kelpie in his

sidecar there
singing in the wind
The girl with blonde hair

blowing back
is smiling sidelong
at the dog

who measures in his
cancelled song
the richness of the instant

And who among you
cruising by
would still deny

the fact of heaven?
If dogs have souls
and God's tattooed

and every angel
has blonde hair
streaming from a helmet

Unknown photographer, *On Our Honeymoon* 1919 (Hugo Throssell and his wife;
Hugo is sitting on a motorcycle); sepia-toned photograph; Papers of Katharine
Prichard, 1851–1970; Manuscripts Collection; MS 6201/1/14

Sheepdogs (Part IV from *Works and Days*)
David Campbell

First dog I had was the dad's, I inherited him
With a mob of stubborn wethers. Don was good on one side.
He'd work out of sight till noon over logs and boulders
And keep sheep propping; then vanish. Times I could have cried.

Peter arrived like a white-eyed bear in a box.
With ewes and lambs he'd move out nice and wide
And freeze when they broke. A collie, he picked up burr.
You could talk to that dog all day till the day he died.

I bought old Choc from a shearer. He knew the answers—
Or so they said and he thought—but tan his hide,
And he worked all day in the dust, eyes on you, smiling.
'Speak up!' and he barked—and nipped a hock on the side.

Pastoral

AUSTRALIA

PARTICULARS AT GOVERNMENT, SHIPPING & TRAVEL OFFICES

AUSTRALIAN NATIONAL
PUBLICITY ASSOCIATION
RAILWAY BUILDING, FLINDERS STREET, MELBOURNE

Walking
Jenny Greve

Only an ordinary suburb—
nothing flash.
Ordinary people, living ordinary lives.

Everyday they take their dogs
for a walk around the circular block.

Girls, boys, couples and lovers.

A grand procession of people and dogs
of all shapes and sizes.

The woman sits at her window
and watches—
this ritual, this joy.

This simple pleasure of walking dogs.

Bruce Howard (b.1936), *On a Bicycle Built for ?* 1981; gelatin silver photograph;
30.3 x 40.5 cm; Pictures Collection; nla.pic-an24986517. Courtesy of Bruce
Howard and The Herald & Weekly Times Pty Ltd

Freedom
Oodgeroo Noonuccal

For Vivian Charles

Brumby on the wide plain,
All men out to break you,
My warm fellow-feeling
Hopes they never take you!

Dingo on the lone ridge,
Fleeing as you spy them,
Every hand against you,
May you still defy them!

All things wild and tameless,
Hunted down and hated,
Something in my wild heart
With your own is mated.

Dingo, wild bushranger,
Brumby that they ban so,
May you still outmatch them,
May you foil the man-foe!

June Orford (b.1946), *Victorian Dingo Society Members and Dingoes at the World Environment Day Rally, Melbourne, 6 June 2004* (detail); coloured digital photograph; Pictures Collection; nla.pic-vn3146221. Courtesy of June Orford

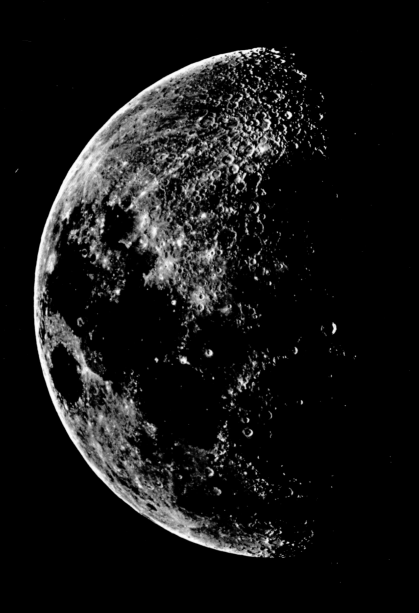

The Dog in the Moon
Henry Lawson

In the days of your childhood, when Granny was there,
And all things were truthful, and all things were fair;
You believed that your sin would be punished right soon—
You believed in the tale of the Man in the Moon.

And for picking up sticks on a Sunday, we knew,
He was sent to the Moon. But his dog followed too.
The master's been dead for full many a June,
But his old dog still mourns him—the Dog in the Moon.

If you do not believe me—and people are dull—
Just seek the right place when the moon is at full.
And you'll hear the dogs howling a dolorous tune—
'Tis the Earth dogs that answer the Dog in the Moon.

Unknown photographer, *Photograph of the Moon Taken with the Great Melbourne Telescope, Moon's Age 9 Days 0 Hours* 1880s; albumen photograph; 24.4 x 20.1 cm Pictures Collection; nla.pic-an24599057

Unolympic Effort
Gloria Yates

I ran round the house
3 times this morning
to impress the dog
it's a small house
but he's a small dog
it was my personal best
and he WAS impressed.

Next event:
belly-tickling.

VADA.
BORN 19TH MAY 1903.
DIED 24TH OCT. 1910.
"SHE WAS A GOOD DOG, AND A FAIR DOG,
CAN THERE MORE BE SAID".

Rex Nan Kivell (1898–1977), *Vada's Tombstone, Dog's Cemetery, Monrant Gardens, Part of the WWI New Zealand First General Hospital at Brockenhurst, Hampshire, UK* 1918?; b&w, nitrate negative; Pictures Collection; nla.pic-vn3318708

A Dog's Elegy
Les Murray

The civil white-pawed dog who'd strain
to make speech-like sounds to his humans
lies buried in the soil of a slope
that he'd tear down on his barking runs.

He hated thunder and gunshot
and would charge off to restrain them.
A city dog too alive for backyards,
we took him from the pound's Green Dream

but now his human name melts off him;
he'll rise to chase fruit bats and bees;
the coral tree and the African tulip
will take him up, and the prickly tea trees.

Our longhaired cat who mistook him
for an Alsatian flew up there full tilt
and teetered in top twigs for eight days
as a cloud, distilling water with its pelt.

The cattle suspect the Dog lives
but three kangaroos stood in our pasture
this daybreak, for the first time in memory,
eared gazing wigwams of fur.

A Boy and a Dog

Marty Hale

I want my boy to have a dog
Or maybe, two or three,
He'll learn from them much easier
Than he would learn from me.

A dog will show him how to love
And bear no grudge or hate,
I'm not so good at that myself
But dogs will do it straight.

I want my boy to have a dog
To be his pal and friend,
So he may learn that friendship
Is faithful to the end.

There never yet has been a dog
Who learned to double cross
Nor catered to you when you won
Or dropped you when you lost.

Raymond de Berquelle (b.1933), *Boy with Black Dog, Surry Hills, Sydney, 1965*
gelatin silver photograph; 27.3 x 36.7 cm; Pictures Collection; nla.pic-an24912751
Courtesy of Raymond de Berquelle

'Retrieving passionate sticks'
Elizabeth Lawson

Retrieving passionate sticks from pond-slime
the retriever believes solid
the waterlilies,
threshes inglorious green
for dry land,
with sheer plod
puzzles his abashed intellect,
sinks (forgiving)
to dogpaddle.

John Flynn (1880–1951), *Drinking Water* 1926; hand-coloured lantern slide:
8.2 x 8.2 cm; Pictures Collection; nla.pic-an24527118. Courtesy of Frontier Services

Workin' Dogs in the City

Andrew Burke

Two dogs tethered to the tray
of a city ute
bring out your sympathy:

    that they can't run
    from side to side
    barking their fool heads off,

    that they can't jump down
    and piss immediately
    on the tyres of fellow vehicles,

    that they can't round-up chooks
    and all creatures great and small
    at journey's end,

    that their spit can't fly
    onto the windscreens of
    traffic on the open road …

These two—part Kelpie, part Heeler—
stand glumly, heads down, like
stock going to the butcher's block.

As they pause at the traffic lights
where we wait at kerbside
they herd sheep into your top paddock

like all your former workin' dogs
who ran and jumped,
their sheepshit paws smudging

that smell of Town from you,
that City Life away from you.

Jeff Carter (b.1928), *Drover, Graham Mansell, Deniliquin, New South Wales, February 2007*
coloured photograph; 42.8 x 28.0 cm; Pictures Collection; nla.pic-vn3970413
Courtesy of Jeff Carter

The Cattle-Dog's Death

Henry Lawson

The plains lay bare on the homeward route,
And the march was heavy on man and brute;
For the Spirit of Drought was on all the land,
And the white heat danced on the glowing sand.

The best of our cattle-dogs lagged at last,
His strength gave out ere the plains were passed,
And our hearts grew sad when he crept and laid
His languid limbs in the nearest shade.

He saved our lives in the years gone by,
When no one dreamed of the danger nigh,
And the treacherous blacks in the darkness crept
On the silent camp where the drovers slept.

'The dog is dying,' a stockman said,
As he knelt and lifted the shaggy head;
''Tis a long day's march ere the run be near,
And he's dying fast; shall we leave him here?'

But the super cried, 'There's an answer there!'
As he raised a tuft of the dog's grey hair;
And, strangely vivid, each man descried
The old spear-mark on the shaggy hide.

We laid a 'bluey' and coat across
The camping pack of the lightest horse,
And raised the dog to his deathbed high,
And brought him far 'neath the burning sky.

At the kindly touch of the stockmen rude
His eyes grew human with gratitude;
And though we parched in the heat that fags,
We gave him the last of the water-bags.

The 'super's' daughter we knew would chide
If we left the dog in the desert wide;
So we brought him far o'er the burning sand
For a parting stroke of her small white hand.

But long ere the station was seen ahead,
His pain was o'er, for the dog was dead;
And the folks all knew by our looks of gloom
'Twas a comrade's corpse that we carried home.

(pp.28–29)
S.T. Gill (1818–1880), *Going to Work* 1850s; watercolour; 24.9 x 33.4 cm
Pictures Collection; nla.pic-an2381127

Stray Dog

Jim Grahame

He followed me from town one day,
    A footsore, weary stray;
And though the road was furnace-hot
    He still limped on my way.
I think he'd been a drover's dog—
    A canine class apart—
He guards the hens and trails the horse
    And sleeps beneath the cart.

He has no quarrel with the cat,
    Shows no desire to roam,
But like my ageing human friends
    He makes himself at home.
He's not a humble kind of dog,
    And does not cringe or quail
Or court my smile or fear my frown,
    And seldom wags his tail.

No snarling blusterer is he,
    But a lone muffled bark
Warns him who enters my domain
    Unbidden in the dark.
Then, bristles up and eye alert,
    He stalks the visitor,
His muzzle at the stranger's heels
    As he walks on before.

He is a trusty, silent friend,
    With eyes that see afar
And ears attuned for distant sounds,
    The way most bush dogs are.
There's just one thing that troubles me—
    No soft food will he eat:
He's from the land of wool and hide
    And meat and meat and meat.

A Dog, a Horse, a Man
K. Collopy

In dawn's grey ghostly light three figures stand
In a ploughed field; black shadows on the grey,
Time-fixed in living stone; the man's gaunt hand
Laid on the steaming withers of the bay,
The dog that stands behind his master's heels,
Covered in mud. In this late-ravished field
Where like a ghost the shape of morning steals
Through bush and fence, by God's white hand revealed
Of dawn and grace, long moon-drugged shadows grip
The silver group, and silver now the sun
Peeps through the river-trees. Long decades run
And wise old words slip lightly from earth's lip,
Yet ages past a scene like this began
Which we see now—a dog, a horse, a man.

Unknown photographer, *'Tis a Hot Day on Patrol and Water is Scarce* c.1935
glass negative; 16.4 x 11.9 cm; Pictures Collection; nla.pic-vn3298444

Nine Miles from Gundagai

Jack Moses

I've done my share of shearing sheep,
    Of droving and all that,
And bogged a bullock-team as well,
    On a Murrumbidgee flat.
I've seen the bullock stretch and strain,
    And blink his bleary eye,
And the dog sit on the tucker box,
    Nine miles from Gundagai.

I've been jilted, jarred, and crossed in love,
    And sand-bagged in the dark,
Till if a mountain fell on me
    I'd treat it as a lark.
It's when you've got your bullocks bogged
    That's the time you flog and cry,
And the dog sits on the tucker box,
    Nine miles from Gundagai.

We've all got our little troubles,
    In life's hard, thorny way.
Some strike them in a motor car
    And others in a dray.
But when your dog and bullocks strike,
    It ain't no apple pie,
And the dog sat on the tucker box,
    Nine miles from Gundagai.

But that's all past and dead and gone,
  And I've sold the team for meat,
And perhaps, some day where I was bogged,
  There'll be an asphalt street.
The dog, ah! well he got a bait,
  And thought he'd like to die,
So I buried him in the tucker box,
  Nine miles from Gundagai.

A Dog's View
C. J. Dennis

I'm only just a common racing dog,
    Simple in habit, and my diet's plain.
I have never had a longing for the grog
    That some men seem to need, more vim to gain.
And I have heard it said of such a one,
    Who in his swilling emulates the hogs:
'He's boozing day and night: he's getting done.
    Poor man,' they say: 'he's going to the dogs.'

But now 'tis threatened that a dog should win
    A newer culture and a swifter pace
By taking to the whisky and the gin,
    That he may wax more reckless in the race.
And we, who hitherto have been content
    With just a lap of water and a rub,
Will soon enough contract that human bent
    Of knocking off and going to the pub.

And then, who knows? Some badly balanced pup,
    Weak-willed, and too intent on hectic joys,
Will learn too soon the way to liquor up
    And have a jolly evening with the boys.
And we shall say of such a one, in blame:
    'It's quite all right to have one now and then;
But he has overdone this drinking game.
    Poor dog,' we'll say: 'He's going to the men.'

Part of ephemera material on greyhound racing collected by the National Library of Australia.
Ephemera Collection; nla.aus-vn3296627-1. © 1938 EMI Allans Music Australia Pty Limited.
International copyright secured. All rights reserved. Used by permission

OFFICIAL PROGRAMME

2/-

N.S.W NATIONAL COURSING ASSOCIATION LIMITED

at WENTWORTH PARK *Oval* GLEBE

THE MECCA OF GREYHOUND RACING

N·C·A

WENTWORTH PARK

PADDOCK

LEGED

WEDNESDAY NIGHT

4th NOVEMBER, 1953

True Lap Dancing

Michael Leunig

(above)
Michael Leunig (b.1945), *True Lap Dancing*, reproduced from *The Age*, 5 March 1999
Courtesy of Michael Leunig

(opposite)
Regis Lansac (b.1947), *Portrait of Louis Nowra with His Chihuahua* 1986; gelatin silver photograph on fibre base paper; 40.5 x 30.3 cm; Pictures Collection; nla.pic-an21898670. Courtesy of Regis Lansac

The Lares
Jemal Sharah

It dates back to the Etruscans, the custom
of household gods; before the tribes of our ancestors
overran Europe, each family
had its guardians. The Romans took it on;
and we, too, have our own: the dog.

Like the Latins', our lives are structured round him.
We invoke him on waking, on going to bed;
on leaving the house we also address him.
He is our conscience, our sense of responsibility:
it is he we go home to, he who hinders our holidays.

His needs persuade us out into the air
in winter's cold and summer's stickiness.
From each meal he takes his propitiation,
the last pieces from each dish. (In return
he barks all day at neighbours, passers-by.)

Dogs are the dumb chroniclers
of the familiar; like Lares, they remind of past events.
Ours saw out an owner's, my brother's, death;
our move from Canberra; and returned from abduction.
It is pets, not parents, shellshocked children cry for.

It wasn't accidental that the Lares
were always shown beside a dog—
'symbol of vigilance and fidelity'.
The Romans understood dogs—from the matron's pet
preserved in fresco, to carved stone hunting hounds,
or the mosaic in the entrance,
the ominous message, 'Beware of the Dog', belied
by the artist's rendition: the frisk
and mock-growling of the dog dancing around him,
its ecstatic wriggle of welcome.

Through history dogs have created normality
in art: the tail which disappears
beneath the last Supper's tablecloth, the pup
pressed to the knight's stone feet upon the tomb.
They are domestic gods—the humble, the ordinary.

Endlessly loyal, they're the ultimate innocents:
more dependent than a child, though their lives
are more separate. Yet dogs have style—
stretched in the sun, inspecting a flea, a paw,
they always rouse a smile.

(pp. 44–45)
Donald Friend (1915–1989), *Dalmation Dog*; Illustrated manuscripts and diaries of
Donald Friend, 1930–1988; Manuscripts Collection; MS 5959/46/241

Acknowledgments

The National Library of Australia wishes to acknowledge the following:

page 3
'My Dog' by Jack Davis, from *The First-born and Other Poems* by Jack Davis (Sydney: Angus & Robertson, 1970). By arrangement with the licensor, The Estate of Jack Davis, c/- Curtis Brown (Aust) Pty Ltd.

page 4
'Relativity' by William Hart-Smith, from *Australian Verse: An Oxford Anthology* edited by John Leonard (Melbourne: Oxford University Press, 1998).

page 7
'the visitor' by Miriel Lenore, from *A Girl's Best Friend: The Meaning of Dogs in Women's Lives* edited by Jan Fook and Renate Klein (Melbourne: Spinifex Press Pty Ltd, 2001). Reproduced with permission from Spinifex Press. First published in *A Girl's Best Friend: The Meaning of Dogs in Women's Lives* (2001).

page 9
'Dogs and God' by Geoff Page, from *Agnostic Skies* by Geoff Page (Carlton, Vic.: Five Island Press, 2006). Courtesy of Geoff Page.

page 10
'Sheepdogs' (Part IV from 'Works and Days') by David Campbell, from *David Campbell Poems* edited by Leonie Kramer (Sydney, NSW: HarperCollins Publishers Australia, 1989). Courtesy of HarperCollins Publishers Australia.

page 13
'Walking' by Jenny Greve, from *Dog Talk: A Collection of Dog Related Poems and Prose* by Jenny Greve (Geelong, Vic.: J. Greve, 1993).

page 14
'Freedom' by Oodgeroo Noonuccal, from *My People*, 4th edn, by
Oodgeroo of the tribe Noonuccal (Milton: John Wiley & Sons, 2008).
Reproduced by permission of John Wiley & Sons, Australia.

page 17
'The Dog in the Moon' by Henry Lawson, from *A Fantasy of Man:
Henry Lawson Completed Works, 1901–1922* compiled and edited by
Leonard Cronin (Sydney: Lansdowne, 1984). Courtesy of New Holland
Publishers Australia.

page 18
'Unolympic Effort' by Gloria Yates, from *Ozpoet: The Definitive Gateway
to Contemporary Australian Poetry*, electronic resource (Sydney: Gillian
Savage, c.1999–2002). Courtesy of Gloria Yates' family.

page 21
'A Dog's Elegy' by Les Murray from *Collected Poems* by Les Murray
(Melbourne: Black Inc., 2006). Courtesy of Margaret Connolly & Associates.

page 22
'A Boy and a Dog' by Marty Hale, from *Dog Lovers' Poems: A Collection
of Prose and Verse* compiled by Jeff Kennett (Melbourne: Information
Australia, 2000).

page 25
'Retrieving Passionate Sticks' by Elizabeth Lawson, from *The Phoenix
Review*, no. 1, Summer 1986/7 edited by David Brooks (Canberra: David
Brooks in association with the English Department of the Australian
National University, 1986/7). Courtesy of Elizabeth Lawson.

page 26
'Workin' Dogs in the City' by Andrew Burke, from *Whispering Gallery*
by Andrew Burke (Cotteslowe, WA: Sunline Press, 2001). Courtesy of
Andrew Burke.

page 30
'The Cattle Dog's Death' by Henry Lawson, from
*A Camp-fire Yarn: Henry Lawson Complete Works,
1885–1900*, compiled and edited by Leonard Cronin
(Sydney: Lansdowne, 1984). Courtesy of New Holland
Publishers Australia.

page 32
'Stray Dog' by Jim Grahame, from *The Bulletin* (Sydney:
Australian Consolidated Press), 19 April 1944.

page 35
'A Dog, a Horse, a Man' by K. Collopy, from *The Bulletin*,
(Sydney: Australian Consolidated Press), 14 March 1945.

page 36
'Nine Miles from Gundagai' by Jack Moses, from
Nine Miles from Gundagai (Sydney, NSW: Angus and
Robertson, 1944).

page 38
'A Dog's View' by C.J. Dennis, viewed 20 June 2008 at
www.middlemiss.org/lit/authors/denniscj/newspapers/
herald/1932/works/dogsview.html, appeared in the
Herald, 27 January 1932.

page 40
'True Lap Dancing' by Michael Leunig, from *The Age*,
5 March 1999.

page 42
'The Lares' by Jemal Sharah, from *Family Ties: Australian
Poems of the Family* edited by Jennifer Strauss (Melbourne:
Oxford University Press, 1998). Courtesy of Jemal Sharah.

Francis Reiss (b.1927), *Paddy Japaljarri Stewart from the Warlukurlangu Artists Aboriginal Association at the Yuendumu Art Centre, Yuendumu, 2003*; Pictures Collection; nla.pic-vn3308281. Courtesy of Paddy Japaljarri Stewart, Chairman, Warlukurlangu Artists Aboriginal Association, Photograph courtesy of Francis Reiss